STAR WARS®

JOURNEY THROUGH SPACE

Written by Ryder Windham

Senior Editor Tori Kosara
Designer Mark Richards
Pre-production Producer Marc Staples
Senior Producer Alex Bell
Managing Editor Laura Gilbert
Managing Art Editor Maxine Pedliham
Art Director Lisa Lanzarini
Publisher Julie Ferris
Publishing Director Simon Beecroft

For Lucasfilm
Executive Editor Jonathan W. Rinzler
Art Director Troy Alders
Story Group Rayne Roberts, Pablo Hidalgo, Leland Chee

Reading Consultant
Dr. Linda Gambrell, PhD

First published in the United States in 2015 by
DK Publishing
4th Floor, 345 Hudson Street, New York 10014

10 9 8 7 6 5 4 3 2 1
001-SD173-Feb/15

Page design Copyright © 2015 Dorling Kindersley Limited
A Penguin Random House Company

Published in Great Britain by Dorling Kindersley Limited.

A catalog record for this book
is available from the Library of Congress.

ISBN: 978-1-4654-3389-3 (Hardback)
ISBN: 978-1-4654-3390-9 (Paperback)
Printed and bound in China by South China Printing Company Ltd.

www.starwars.com
www.dk.com

A WORLD OF IDEAS:
SEE ALL THERE IS TO KNOW

Contents

Planet Profiles

Come on a journey through space to the *Star Wars* galaxy. It is far, far away. There are many stars and planets in this galaxy. Each planet is different. Let's take a closer look.

TATOOINE

DESERT PLANET

Number of Suns:	2
Number of Moons:	3
Population:	200,000
Environment:	desert
Climate:	hot and dry
Famous for:	podracing

HOTH

ICE PLANET

Number of Suns:	1
Number of Moons:	3
Population:	fewer than 10
Environment:	icy
Climate:	cold and snowy
Famous for:	large glaciers

KASHYYYK

FOREST PLANET

Number of Suns:	1
Number of Moons:	3
Population:	**56 million**
Environment:	**tropical forest**
Climate:	**warm and wet**
Famous for:	**fierce warriors**

MUSTAFAR

VOLCANO PLANET

Number of Suns:	1
Number of Moons:	0
Population:	**20,000**
Environment:	**volcanic**
Climate:	**extremely hot**
Famous for:	**metal mines**

Coruscant

Coruscant is the most important planet. It is covered by one enormous city.

All the buildings in the city are gleaming skyscrapers.

Many important people live here.
Powerful Jedi Knights call this
place home.
The Jedi High Council has
important meetings in a temple
on Coruscant.

ADI GALLIA

Adi knows many important people who can help the Council.

SAESEE TIIN

Saesee has a special skill. He sees things that have not yet happened.

The Jedi High Council

YODA

Jedi Master Yoda leads the High Council. He is very powerful.

KI-ADI-MUNDI

Ki-Adi-Mundi is one of the most experienced members on the council.

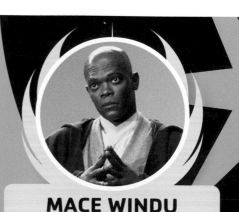

MACE WINDU

Mace is wise. He joined the Council at a very young age.

YADDLE

Yaddle is a very wise Jedi Master. She is also kind and patient.

YARAEL POOF

Yarael likes to play mind tricks on the other Council members.

The Jedi High Council members meet at the Jedi Temple, which is on the planet Coruscant.
The most skilled and wise Jedi sit on the Council. There are always 12 seats. If a member dies or leaves, a new member is chosen to replace them.

OPPO RANCISIS

Oppo is a traditional Jedi. He does not like to try modern ways.

PLO KOON

Plo has great fighting skills. He is also an amazing pilot.

EETH KOTH

Eeth is highly intelligent. He always uses his mind for good.

Naboo

People and Gungans live
on the planet Naboo.
The people live in beautiful
cities on the land.

The Gungans live in
underwater cities.
They can walk
on land, too,
although some
are a bit clumsy!
Jar Jar Binks
is a Gungan.

Tatooine

The planet Tatooine is
covered by a dusty desert.
Two suns shine in the sky so
it is very hot.
There is not much water on
this planet.

Tatooine is a meeting place.
Space travelers visit the planet
from all over the galaxy.
People come from near and far
to watch a high-speed sport
called podracing.

Kamino

Water flooded all the land on the planet Kamino.

So the Kaminoans built their cities on strong metal poles that stick up above the water.

Kaminoans are very tall with long, thin necks. They ride winged beasts to fly and swim around their watery planet.

Geonosis

Geonosis is not a good
place to be captured.
Prisoners are forced to fight
huge monsters in special arenas.
The fights are dangerous.

Scary beasts are brought
from other planets
to the arenas.
The Geonosians look
like insects.
They watch the fights.

Geonosian Arena Beasts

The beasts used in the arena on Geonosis are from far away planets. Each creature is dangerous in its own way.

REEK

HOMEWORLD: Ylesia

HEIGHT: 2.24 m (7 ft 4 in)

DIET: Herbivore (plant-eater) but forced to eat meat

HABITAT: Grassland

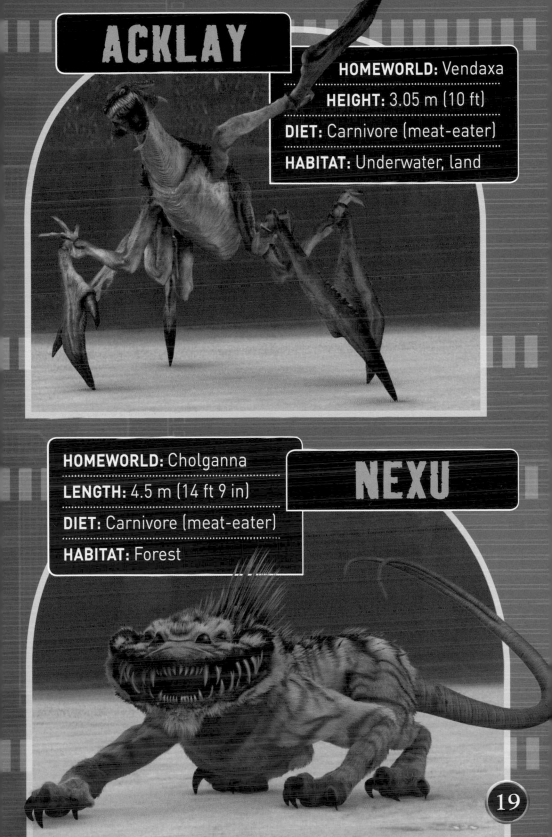

ACKLAY

HOMEWORLD: Vendaxa

HEIGHT: 3.05 m (10 ft)

DIET: Carnivore (meat-eater)

HABITAT: Underwater, land

HOMEWORLD: Cholganna

LENGTH: 4.5 m (14 ft 9 in)

DIET: Carnivore (meat-eater)

HABITAT: Forest

NEXU

Kashyyyk

Kashyyyk is a world of giant
trees and shallow lakes.

It is home to the Wookiees,
including Chewbacca and Tarfful.

Wookiees are tall and have
lots of shaggy fur.

They talk in grunts and roars.

Utapau

The planet Utapau
has lots of deep holes.
The Utapauns dig
tunnels through
rocks to join
the holes.
There are other
creatures on the planet.

Creatures called Utai live
in holes in the ground.
Enormous lizards called
varactyl wander around
the rocky land.
They are good climbers.
The Utai ride the varactyl.

Mustafar

The red planet of Mustafar
is a very hot place.
It is covered in fiery volcanoes.
Hot, melted rock called lava
flows from the volcanoes.
The sky is filled with black
smoke that blocks out the sun.

Polis Massa

The space rock known as
Polis Massa has a medical center.
This is where space travelers
can go if they are sick.
The doctors are helped by
special robots called droids.

Medical Droids

Different kinds of droids work at the medical center on Polis Massa. Each robot has a special job to do.

2-1B DROID

A 2-1B droid does lots of things. This robot can give patients check-ups. It speaks with a calm voice.

DD-13 MEDICAL ASSISTANT DROID

These droids can give humans replacement parts, such as hands. The new robotic piece is called a cybernetic part.

GH-7 DROID

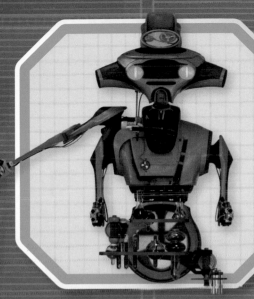

- These droids have many skills. They are good at giving blood tests. These tests help to find out what is making a patient sick.

MIDWIFE DROID

Midwife droids are experts at delivering babies. They make sure that the babies are safe and healthy.

FX-6 DROID

- It is not always easy to tell what is wrong with a patient. An FX-6 droid can help doctors figure out what the patient needs.

Yavin 4

The moon Yavin 4 is covered
in thick jungle.
The ruins of very old buildings
called temples rise above the trees.

At one time, the soldiers
who lived on Yavin 4 kept watch
for enemy starships from
the tops of the tallest temples.

Tour the Great Temple on Yavin 4

by our Special Galaxy Reporter

There are ancient temples on Yavin 4. This moon is very far away and hard to get to. Only plants and animals live here. Not many people have seen these special buildings.

The Great Temple is tucked away deep in the jungle. It takes a long time to trek through the hot, sticky forest.

The temple is huge! Its old bricks are covered in large, twisted vines. Soft green moss also grows on the walls.

Ancient warriors built the Great Temple more than 5,000 years ago.

The Great Temple

Starships inside the temple

Soldiers once lived here. The soldiers used the inside of the temple to keep their starships safe. There were also rooms where they could eat or sleep.

Today, no one uses the temple or lives there. The Great Temple is an old but amazing building to see and explore.

Hoth

The ice planet Hoth is very cold.
Here, the land is covered in snow
and ice.
On Hoth, people ride around
on large beasts called tauntauns.

Wampa ice creatures live
in ice caves.

They hang the animals that
they catch from the cave roof.

Once, a wampa even captured
a Jedi Knight!

Dagobah

The planet Dagobah
is covered in thick forests
and swampy land.
The air is steamy, and it rains a lot.
There are many deadly creatures
and poisonous plants.

The Jedi Master Yoda went
to hide on Dagobah.
He lived in a small tree house.

Bird's-eye View

Yoda is the only intelligent being that lives on the planet Dagobah. But there are many unique animals, plants, and places to see here.

Gnarltree bridge over lagoon

Sweet water lagoon

Yoda gathers yarum seeds from this part of the forest

Yoda's house
Yoda lives alone in a small house. The house is surrounded by swampland.

Gnarltrees

These trees have large, twisty roots. Gnarltrees grow best in swamps.

Yogurt plants

Cave

Quicksand

DRAGON SNAKE BOG

Jubba birds use mud to make nests in the trees

Dragon snake

A giant beast called a dragon snake lives here. He hides under the water, and waits for his next meal.

Cloud City

Cloud City floats in the skies
of the planet Bespin.
Visitors come to enjoy its
lively shops, restaurants,
and hotels.

Cloud cars fly around the city.

They have room for two passengers.

Endor

The forest moon of the planet
Endor is the home of small,
furry creatures called Ewoks.
They live in the trees and
use simple tools and spears.

At night, Ewoks stay in the
villages that they build high
up in the trees.

We hope you have enjoyed your
tour of the galaxy.

Come back soon!

Glossary

Creature
An animal that is not a human being.

Desert
A dry area of land with little water and few plants.

Droid
A kind of robot.

Galaxy
A group of millions of stars and planets.

Jungle
An area of land with thick forests and lots of plants. Jungles are usually found in tropical (warm, wet) areas.

Planet
A giant ball-shaped rock that goes around a star. Naboo is a planet.

Shallow
Not very deep.

Skyscraper
A very tall building with many stories.

Temple
A building used for religious services.

Volcano
A mountain or hill through which lava comes out.

Index

Guide for Parents

DK Readers is a multi-level interactive reading adventure series for children, developing the habit of reading widely for both pleasure and information. These books have an exciting running text interspersed with a range of reading genres to suit your child's reading ability, as required by the school curriculum. Each book is designed to develop your child's reading skills, fluency, grammar awareness, and comprehension in order to build confidence and engagement when reading.

Ready for a *Beginning to Read Alone* book
YOUR CHILD SHOULD

- be able to read most words without needing to stop and break them down into sound parts.
- read smoothly, in phrases and with expression. By this level, your child will be mostly reading silently.
- self-correct when a word or sentence doesn't sound right.

A valuable and shared reading experience

For many children, reading requires much effort, but adult participation can make this both fun and easier. So here are a few tips on how to use this book with your child.

TIP 1 **Check out the contents together before your child begins:**
- invite your child to check the blurb, contents page, and layout of the book and comment on it.
- ask your child to make predictions about the story.
- talk about the information your child might want to find out.

TIP 2 **Encourage fluent and flexible reading:**
- support your child to read in fluent, expressive phrases, making full use of punctuation and thinking about the meaning.

- help your child learn to read with expression by choosing a sentence to read aloud and demonstrating how to do this.

TIP 3 Indicators that your child is reading for meaning:

- your child will be responding to the text if he/she is self-correcting and varying his/her voice.
- your child will want to chat about what he/she is reading or is eager to turn the page to find out what will happen next.

TIP 4 Chat at the end of each chapter:

- encourage your child to recall specific details after each chapter.
- let your child pick out interesting words and discuss what they mean.
- talk about what each of you found most interesting or most important.
- ask questions about the text. These help to develop comprehension skills and awareness of the language used.

A FEW ADDITIONAL TIPS

- Read to your child regularly to demonstrate fluency, phrasing, and expression; to find out or check information; and for sharing enjoyment.
- Encourage your child to reread favorite texts to increase reading confidence and fluency.
- Check that your child is reading a range of different types of material, such as poems, jokes, and following instructions.

Series consultant, **Dr. Linda Gambrell**, Distinguished Professor of Education at Clemson University, has served as President of the National Reading Conference, the College Reading Association, and the International Reading Association. She is also reading consultant for the **DK Adventures**.

Have you read these other great books from DK?

BEGINNING TO READ ALONE

Join Luke
Skywalker and his
friends as they
save the galaxy.

Meet a band of
rebels, brave
enough to take on
the Empire!

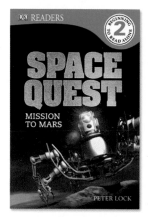

Embark on
a mission to
space, and
explore Mars.

READING ALONE

Discover the
amazing power
of the Force, and
meet Jedi Knights.

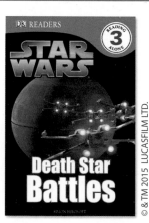

Take a look inside
the Empire's
deadliest weapon,
if you dare!

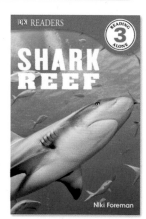

Meet the
sharks who live
on the reef, or
pass through.